SACAJAWEA EXPLORES THE WEST

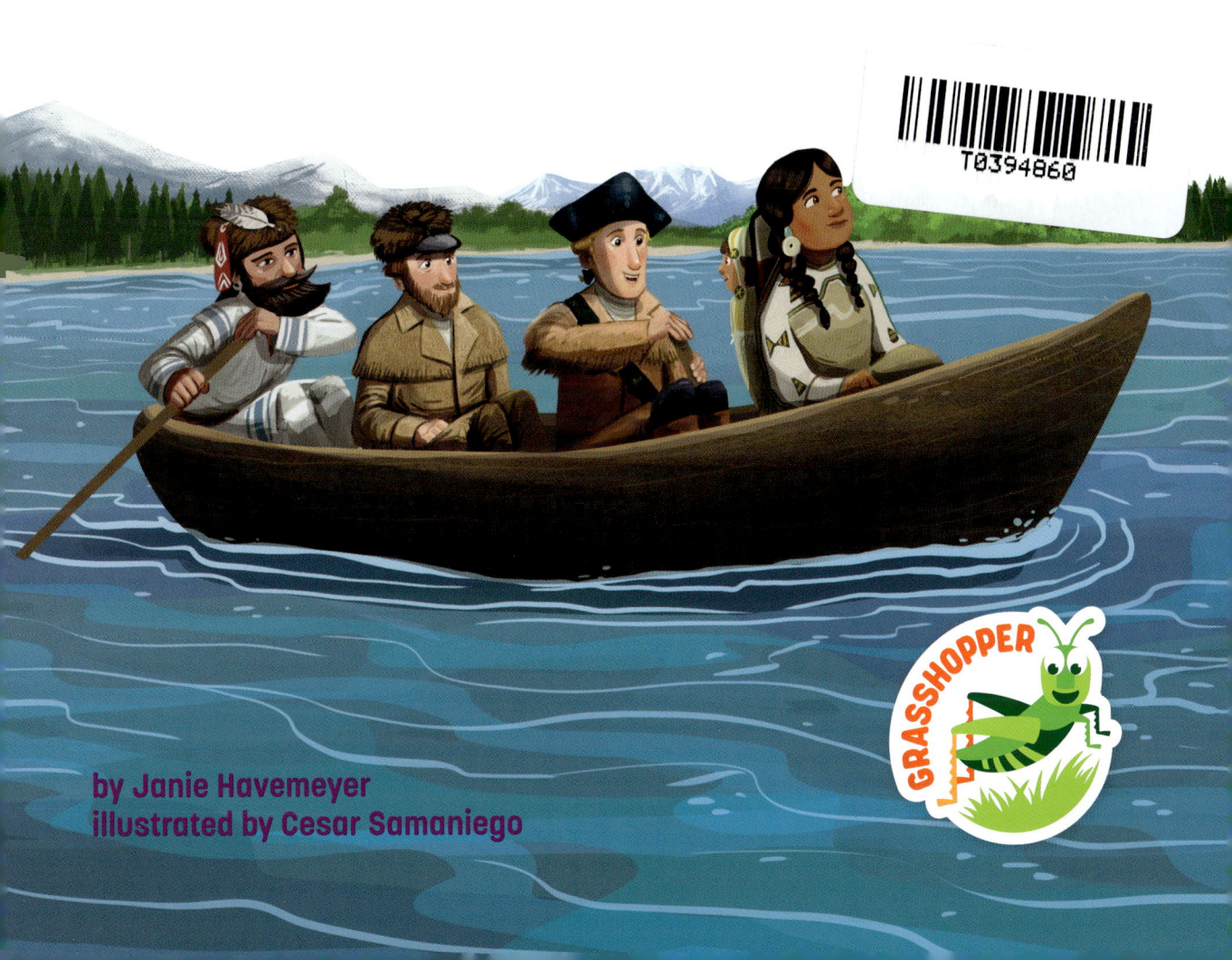

by Janie Havemeyer
illustrated by Cesar Samaniego

GRASSHOPPER

Tools for Parents & Teachers

Grasshopper Books enhance imagination and introduce the earliest readers to fun storylines and illustrations. The easy-to-read text supports early reading experiences with repetitive sentence patterns and sight words.

Before Reading

- Discuss the cover illustration. What do they see?
- Look at the glossary together. Discuss the words.

Read the Book

- Read the book to the child, or have him or her read independently.
- "Walk" through the book and look at the illustrations. Who is the main character? What is happening in the story?

After Reading

- Prompt the child to think more. Ask: How did Sacajawea help the Corps of Discovery travel and explore the West?

Grasshopper Books are published by Jump!
5357 Penn Avenue South
Minneapolis, MN 55419
www.jumplibrary.com

Library of Congress Cataloging-in-Publication Data

Names: Havemeyer, Janie, author. Samaniego, César, 1975- illustrator.
Title: Sacajawea explores the West / by Janie Havemeyer; illustrated by Cesar Samaniego.
Description: Minneapolis, MN: Jump!, Inc., [2025]
Series: Adventurers in history | Includes index.
Audience: Ages 7-10
Identifiers: LCCN 2023054582 (print)
LCCN 2023054583 (ebook)
ISBN 9798892132121 (hardcover)
ISBN 9798892132138 (paperback)
ISBN 9798892132145 (ebook)
Subjects: LCSH: Sacagawea–Juvenile literature. | Lewis and Clark Expedition (1804-1806) –Juvenile literature. | Shoshoni women–Biography–Juvenile literature. | Shoshoni Indians–Biography–Juvenile literature.
Classification: LCC F592.7.S123 H38 2025 (print)
LCC F592.7.S123 (ebook)
DDC 978.004/9745740092 [B] –dc23/eng/20231205
LC record available at https://lccn.loc.gov/2023054582
LC ebook record available at https://lccn.loc.gov/2023054583

Editor: Alyssa Sorenson
Direction and Layout: Anna Peterson
Illustrator: Cesar Samaniego

Printed in the United States of America at Corporate Graphics in North Mankato, Minnesota.

Table of Contents

Guiding the Way

Sacajawea steps into a boat with her two-month-old son. She has lived with the Hidatsa Tribe for years. But now she and her husband are joining a large **expedition**.

It is April 7, 1805. They leave the area now known as North Dakota. The boats head **upstream** on the Missouri River. The group is going west to the Pacific Ocean.

Meriwether Lewis and William Clark lead the group. It is called the **Corps** of Discovery. They want to explore and map the western United States.

Sacajawea and her husband are **interpreters** for the Corps. They will help Lewis and Clark talk with Native Americans they meet on their journey.

William Clark

Meriwether Lewis

7

One day, the group travels on a rough river. Strong winds blow. Sacajawea's boat tips. It fills with water. The men **panic**.

8

Sacajawea thinks fast. She grabs supplies that fell overboard. She saves medicine, **gunpowder**, and clothing. The group needs these to **survive** in the wild.

The Corps travels for months. They go through a valley. Sacajawea knows this place. It is where her tribe, the Lemhi Shoshone, lives.

Sacajawea thinks about the day she was **kidnapped** more than four years ago. She was taken east by the Hidatsa Tribe. Now, the explorers need the Lemhi Shoshone's help.

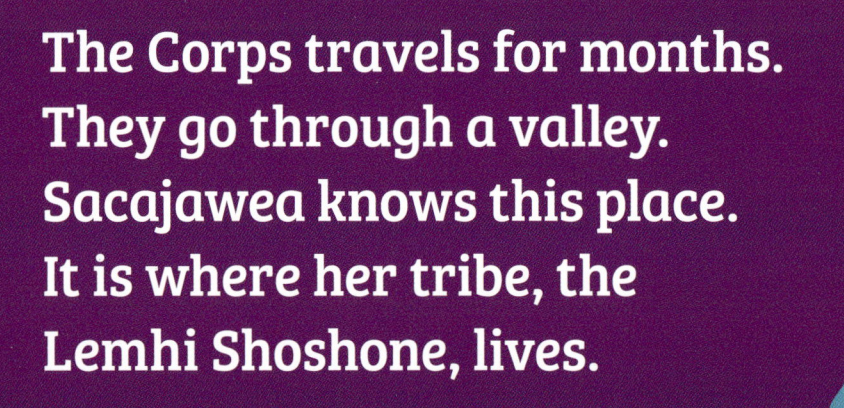

Lewis finds a group of Lemhi Shoshone. He sets up a meeting with their chief. Sacajawea is there to interpret. She knows Chief Cameahwait. He is her brother. She cries with joy when she sees him.

She asks her brother to give the explorers horses. She also asks for people to help guide them over the mountains. Her brother agrees.

The path over the Rocky Mountains is steep. It is cold. There are not enough animals to hunt. Everyone is hungry and weak. Sacajawea points out which plants are safe to eat.

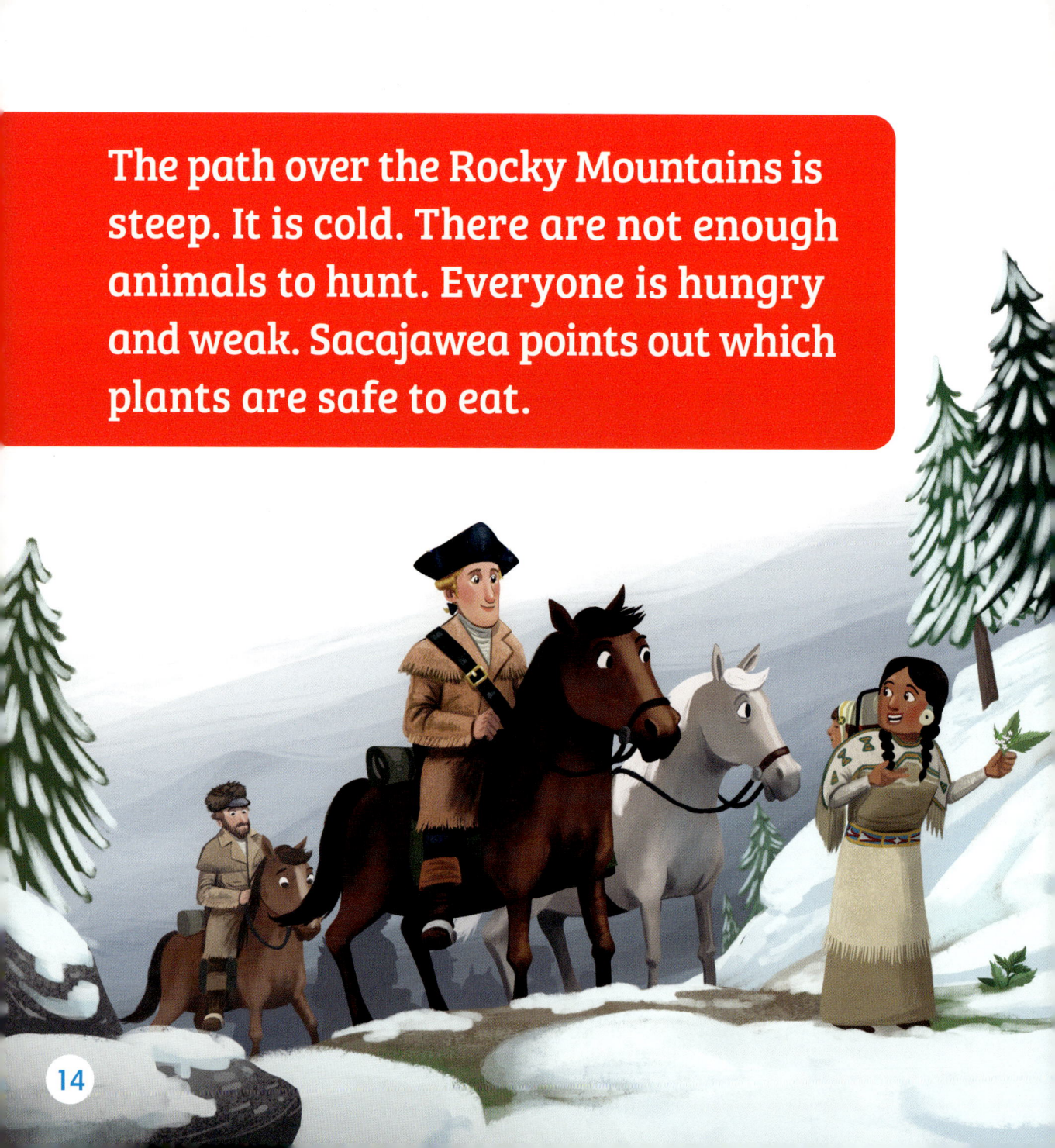

After 11 days, the group makes it over the mountains. They reach a grassy plain in what is now Idaho. The Nez Perce live here. They share food with the explorers.

The explorers build five canoes. Then the Corps paddles farther west. They see many Native Americans. Sacajawea tells the tribes that the explorers are peaceful.

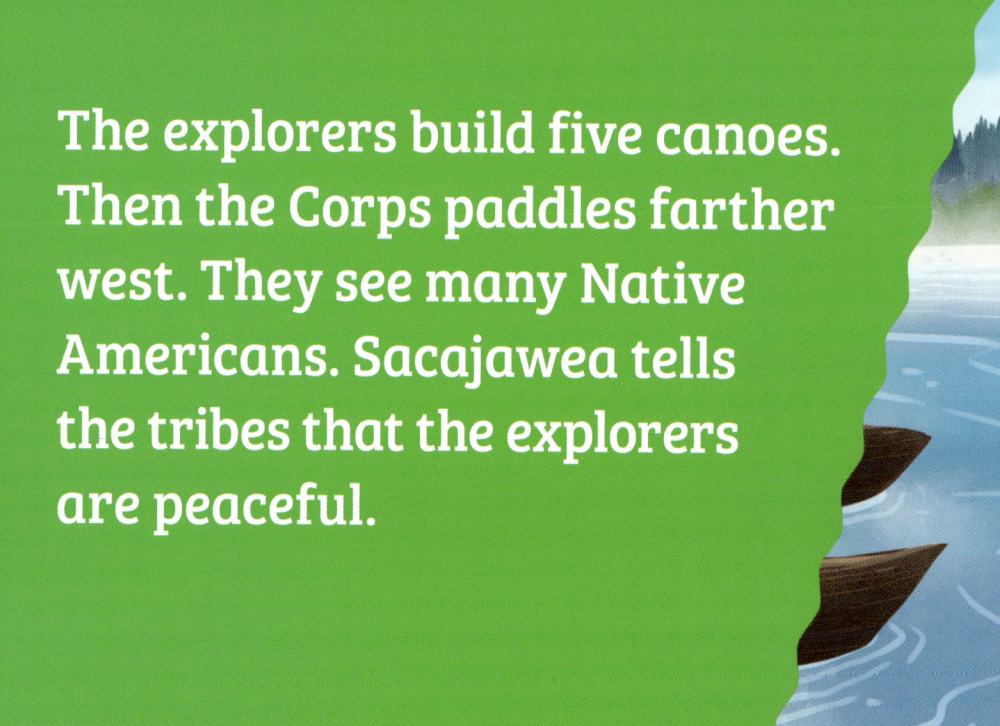

The group reaches the Pacific Coast in November. Sacajawea helps find a good spot to build a camp. They stay through the winter.

In January 1806, some explorers want to go closer to the ocean. Sacajawea begs to go along. They travel for two days. Sacajawea breathes in the salty air. She stares at the blue water. It stretches as far as the eye can see.

Sacajawea has traveled more than 4,000 miles (6,437 kilometers). Lewis and Clark trust and **rely** on her. She has helped them explore the West.

Sacajawea's Timeline

1788
Around this time, Sacajawea is born into the Lemhi Shoshone Tribe in what is now Idaho.

1800
Sacajawea is kidnapped by Hidatsa warriors. She is taken to what is now North Dakota.

May 14, 1804
The Lewis and Clark Expedition begins outside St. Louis, Missouri.

April 7, 1805
Sacajawea joins the expedition.

August 1805
Sacajawea asks the Lemhi Shoshone for horses and guides to travel through the mountains.

May 14, 1805
Sacajawea recues important supplies when they fall out of a boat.

January 8, 1806
Sacajawea sees the Pacific Ocean.

March 23, 1806
Sacajawea and the Corps begin the return journey home.

August 1806
Sacajawea leaves the Corps and returns to the Hidatsa Tribe.

1812
Some historians believe Sacajawea dies of a fever.

Sacajawea's Journey

Sacajawea joined Lewis and Clark when they were in what is now North Dakota. What path did they take west? Take a look!

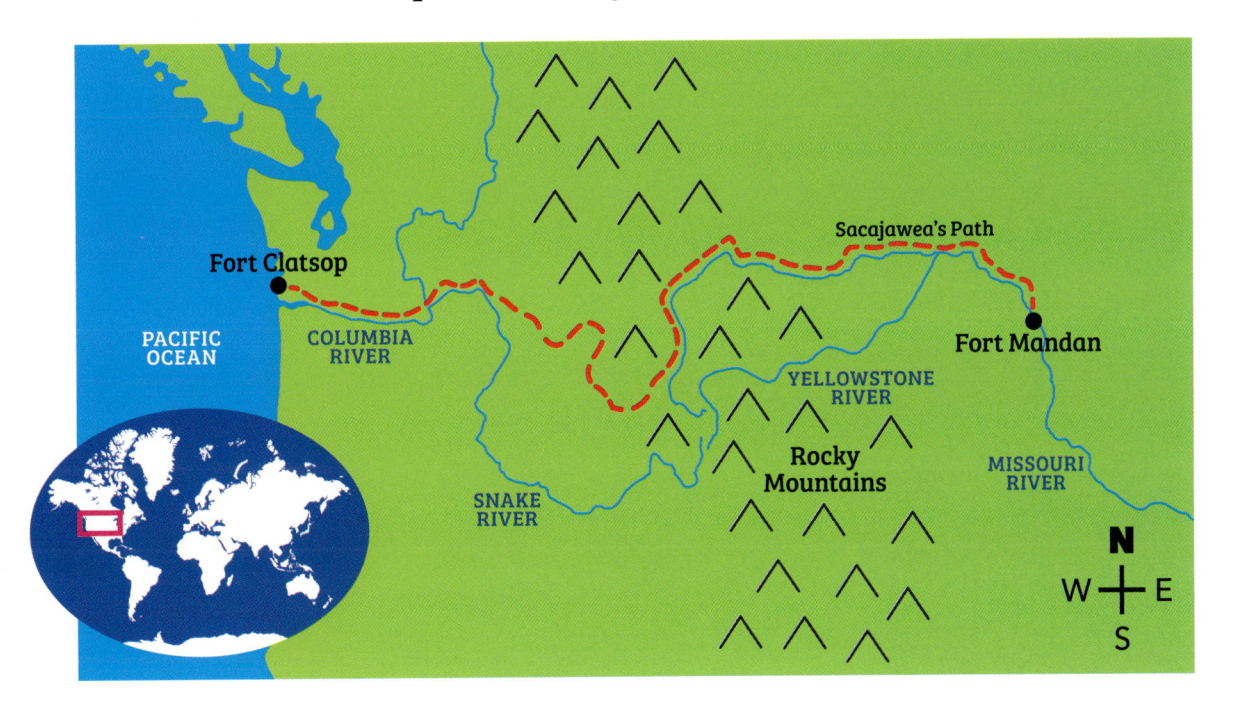

To Learn More

Finding more information is as easy as 1, 2, 3.

❶ Go to www.factsurfer.com

❷ Enter "**Sacajawea**" into the search box.

❸ Choose your book to see a list of websites.

Glossary

corps: A group of people acting together or doing the same thing.

expedition: A journey made for a specific purpose, such as exploration.

gunpowder: A powder that explodes easily and is used in bullets.

interpreters: People who change spoken words from one language into another.

kidnapped: Captured and taken away by force.

panic: To feel sudden, overwhelming fear.

rely: To have trust in or to be dependent on someone.

survive: To stay alive.

upstream: Toward the source of a river.

Index